CHETCO COMMUNITY PUBLIC LIBRARY

3 0010 00099 3835

D0842855

Chetco Community Public Library
405 Alder Street
Brookings, OR 97415

WITHDRAWN

WOLVES

Wolves

DANIEL WOOD

Whitecap Books

Vancouver/Toronto

Chetco Community Public Library
405 Alder Street
Brookings, OR 97415

Copyright © 1994 by Whitecap Books Ltd.
Vancouver/Toronto

Second Printing, 1995

All rights reserved. No part of this publication may be reproduced, stored in
a retrieval system, or transmitted in any form or by any means, electronic,
mechanical, photocopying, recording or otherwise, without prior written
permission of the publisher.

The information in this book is true and complete to the best of our knowledge.
All recommendations are made without guarantee on the part of the author or
Whitecap Books Ltd. The author and publisher disclaim any liability in
connection with the use of this information. For additional information please
contact Whitecap Books Ltd., 351 Lynn Avenue, North Vancouver, B.C., V7J 2C4.

Edited by Elizabeth McLean
Cover design by Steve Penner
Interior design by Margaret Ng
Cover photograph by Peter McLeod/First Light
Maps by Stuart Daniel
Typeset by CompuType

Printed and bound in Canada by D.W. Friesen and Sons Ltd., Altona, Manitoba.

Canadian Cataloguing in Publication Data
Wood, Daniel.
        Wolves
        Includes bibliographical references and index.
        ISBN 1-55110-198-X
    1. Wolves. 2. Wolves—Pictorial works. I. Title.
QL737.C22W66 1994   599.74'442   C94-910415-9

Far across the Tanana, a mile or two to the south of us, a group of wolves were singing. I call it singing, not howling, for that is what it was like. We could distinguish three, perhaps four voices—wavering, ascending in pitch, each one following the other, until they all broke off in a confused chorus. Their voices sank into distant echoes on the frozen river, and began again. A light and uncertain wind was blowing out there, and the sound grew and faded as the air brought it toward us or carried it away southward. It might have come across a thousand years of ice and wind-packed snow, traveling as the light of the stars from a source no longer there.

—John Haines
The Stars, The Snow, The Fire

PREVIOUS PAGE: *A wolf pack is led by a pair of dominant wolves, known in scientific jargon as the ''alpha'' male and ''alpha'' female. The pack maintains a well-established territory, its boundaries regularly marked by the dominant male's urine and the rubbing of scent-glands on convenient natural objects. The size of the territory varies depending on the location and number of prey available. On Vancouver Island, for example, deer are abundant and a pack of ten wolves may occupy just 60 square kilometres (25 square miles). In northern Michigan, a pack of ten may require a territory ten times that size. In northern Alberta, one pack of ten may control 1300 square kilometres (500 square miles).*

C O N T E N T S

INTRODUCTION

SUCCESS OF NATURE, VICTIM OF HISTORY: THE PREDATOR BECAME THE PREY

The wolf—yellow-eyed, loping, relentless, carnivorous—prowls the periphery of human vision, populating the jack-pine forest just beyond the firelight and the myths that darkness fosters. It's not surprising that, through the millenia, people have developed a love-hate relationship with this predator. For wolves—like people—have shared the same territory and many of the same characteristics. The gray wolf (*Canis lupus*) has the largest natural range of any mammal other than its ancient nemesis, *Homo sapiens*. Its sociability was recognized when, about 12 000 years ago, early humans in the Near East domesticated the wolf, making it the predecessor of all 120 species of dogs today. The wolf's allegiance to its pack's leaders, its strong parental sense, its exceptional hunting skills, its poetic howling, even its bloodthirsty nature—occasionally killing for the sake of killing—are mirrors, reflecting the proximity of the primitive in human nature.

PREVIOUS PAGE, LEFT: *Among themselves, wolves are very affectionate—constantly touching other members of the group. Since most packs are composed exclusively of members of a single, extended family—parents, aunts and uncles, half-brothers and sisters, and young pups—the cohesion is genetic as well as behavioral.*

PREVIOUS PAGE, RIGHT: *The female timber wolf weighs about 35 kilograms (75 pounds). The male weighs about 40 kilograms (90 pounds). The wolf's long legs and wide paws provide it with the capacity to chase its prey through deep snow and boggy tundra.*

That is why the wolf features so prominently in the folktales and legends of the northern hemisphere. In 20 000-year-old cave drawings from southern Europe, in accounts from Mesopotamian farmers 7000 years ago, in early Christian demonology, in tales of werewolves from the Middle Ages, in gothic stories like Little Red Riding Hood and The Three Little Pigs, *Canis lupus* gradually assumed its fateful—and undeserved—reputation as Evil Incarnate. Much of this misconception was the result of agrarian European cultures seeking justification for killing an animal that sometimes preyed on their livestock.

In North America, where native hunter-gatherers had no concept of domesticated herds of goats, sheep, or cattle, the wolf assumed a benign, even honored, role: wise, powerful,

LEFT: *The red wolf is nearly extinct as a result of over 100 years of poisoning and hunting by ranchers and farmers. It now survives naturally only in isolated pockets of Texas and Louisiana. Despite occasional suggestions to re-introduce it in some wilderness areas of the U.S. southwest that it once inhabited, lingering anti-wolf attitudes in the region make the prospect unlikely. Attempts have been made to re-introduce the red wolf in the American southeast—with limited success.*

an instinctive hunter, a teacher, in fact, of tactics humans could emulate against buffalo or caribou. But with the arrival in North America of the European colonialists in the 17th century, the extermination of this continent's wolves began. That the wolf has in the last 300 years been eradicated from much of Europe and most of the contiguous 48 American states is a tribute to the power of agricultural societies to conjure up myths and create legislation against the unreal, but imagined, threat of the Big, Bad Wolf huffing and puffing at the door.

The fact is: no animal on earth has been so unfairly maligned or so completely misunderstood.

Originally, the wolf occupied most of North America—from the icy islands of Canada's arctic to the dry, mountainous ravines of central Mexico. The only areas that it never inhabited were the southeast corner of the U.S. and coastal California and Mexico. Across this enormous range, the wolf made regional adaptations to the climate, the terrain, and the available prey. Some zoologists claim that these variations in appearance and behavior have produced 24 subspecies of wolves in North America; others set the number of subspecies at only five.

The timber or gray wolf of the Canadian forest is the largest member of the canine family, which includes coyotes, foxes, dingos, and jackals. Almost three-quarters of a metre (27 inches) tall and two metres (six feet) long, the gray wolf occupies in most of its territory the top of the food chain, rivalled only in the Pacific Northwest by cougars and grizzly bears and in the arctic by polar bears. The timber wolf's mottled, gray-white coat, its long legs, and

its impressive ten-centimetre-wide (four-inch) paws are suited for bushwhacking over crusted snow in pursuit of deer and moose.

The smaller white or subarctic wolf of northern Canada and Alaska depends on its coloration to attack herds of musk ox and caribou in its terrain. Naturalists report that this is the only subspecies of wolf which has not developed an instinctive distrust of man. Patient observers of the white wolf relate incidents of playful pups untying the laces of photographers' boots and adults urinating on human intruders' tent-posts as if to reassert their territorial claims.

The highly endangered red wolf, now isolated in small parts of Louisiana and Texas, is the smallest member of the wolf family. It has developed an unusual ability, sometimes standing on its spindly rear legs to peer across grasslands and swamps, searching for rabbits and rats. The grayish, dry-lands Mexican wolf stands at the threshold of extinction, numbering in the wild fewer than 40.

Beyond these differences, the various subspecies of wolf share a number of similarities, regardless of locale, in social structure, in mating patterns, in parenting, in play, and in hunting techniques. These intimate details are known because, as a result of its long and controversial interaction with humans, the wolf has probably been more intensively studied than any other wild animal on earth. In the last half-century, field naturalists have spent unnumbered hours recording the behavior of North America's wolves. Gradually, the old perceptions have been replaced by information based, not on superstition and fear, but on close observation and analysis.

LEFT: *In European mythology and history, the wolf was often portrayed as the Anti-Christ, epitome of evil. In the 1760s, two wolves—known as the "beasts of Gévaudan"—supposedly killed almost 100 people in southern France. The wolf has been exterminated in most of Europe in the past four centuries. Pockets of wolves survive in mountainous Spain, France, Italy, and forested Finland. The wolf population of Asia has been equally decimated, although substantial numbers remain in remote corners of the Middle East and on the Russian and Mongolian steppes.*

PREVIOUS PAGE: *A gray wolf explores the perimeter of a Canadian pond. Canada is home to 60 000 wolves, inhabiting 90 percent of the entire country. Alaska has about one-tenth the number of wolves in Canada. But hunting and trapping of wolves is still permitted in large parts of these regions— providing subsistence income to rural people.*

Few mammals anywhere are as aware—and as loyal to—their social group as the wolf. Unlike coyotes and foxes, the wolf usually *exists* for its pack. The rare exception is the proverbial "lone wolf"—the runt, the outsider, ostracized from the pack. This wolf may wander ten kilometres (six miles) or 1000 kilometres (600 miles), passing cautiously through the domains of other packs until it finds a mate and begins a new pack. For most wolves, however, their identity begins and ends as part of a cohesive, eight- to fifteen-member pack. The hierarchy of the pack is known to all and reinforced by favors, rituals, nips, and fights. The so-called alpha male and female are the pack's leaders. The subservient members are usually direct descendants of the alpha parents, which means a pack is really one extended family. Some subservient wolves assist in feeding and raising each spring's new batch of pups. All share in hunting duties. All socialize together, snooze together, and often howl together. All pay daily, ritualized allegiance to the group's leaders.

This ability to communicate in a communal group sets the wolf apart from most other North American animals. Lower-ranking younger wolves literally bow before the alpha adults to show their submission. And unlike the dominant adults that urinate with a raised leg, many weaker wolves squat while urinating to minimize the distribution of scent. Most packs have a regular, weaker "baby-sitter" that helps look after the young—and often goes hungry— while the alpha parents are out hunting. In attacks on large prey, the wolf employs a wide variety of group tactics, led initially by the pair of alpha wolves which communicate through vocalizations, facial expressions, and body movements to other pack members.

Another role of the pack is to protect its territory against incursions from other wolves. This strong identity with an established area of land may last for generations. The boundaries of this area are fiercely protected by regular, ritual scent-markings every 100 to 200 metres (or yards) along a perimeter that typically encompasses—depending on the subspecies and the amount of available prey—about 400 square kilometres (150 square miles). The wolves within this area see the local game as "their" prey. Intruding wolves are attacked and, on occasion, killed.

Research has shown the wolf prefers wild game, selecting among ungulates like elk, deer, and mountain sheep where possible, but utilizing a full range of local resources, including bison, seals, beaver, muskrat, voles, waterfowl, fish, garbage, and even berries. But it is the wolf's reputation as a killer of domestic animals that has earned it so much trouble.

At the turn of the century, several American wolves gained notoriety and nicknames for their predation of livestock. One wolf, named "Old Lefty" since it had lost a left paw in a trap, became a legend in Colorado, killing, it is said, 384 head of livestock in 1913. And "Three Toes," another maimed wolf, reportedly took $50 000 worth of cattle in its time. Despite the fact that there have been no recorded human deaths from wolf attacks in North America, a persistent fear of wolves and the occasional livestock-killing lent credence to the long-held view that nothing could prevent wolf predation except mass slaughter.

Between 1630 and 1960 in North America, a systematic eradication of the wolf population followed the westward expansion of the frontier. At first, as had happened earlier in

LEFT: *The wolf has developed the capacity to survive in the most inhospitable of climates. These wolves of the high arctic endure several winter months of perpetual darkness. Even in February when the sun returns to the north, temperatures of -40° C (-40° F) and bitter winds are common. Other wolves are at home in the heat of the desert and the dampness of a humid Gulf Coast swamp. With such a range, the wolf is probably the most adaptable and successful non-human predator on earth.*

PREVIOUS PAGE: *The gray wolf once ranged over half the earth, almost everywhere in the northern hemisphere except Central America, North Africa, and Southeast Asia. Only the lion—until prehistoric times— had a greater range among mammals. Gradually, the lion disappeared from both the Americas and much of Asia. Today, the wolf is second in territorial range to only one other mammal: humans.*

Europe, wolves were killed by farmers and herders whenever the animals trespassed on agricultural land. As settlement spread west, early explorers reported that the number of wolves on the Great Plains rivalled the number of buffalo. Following the explorers, farmers, cattlemen, and trappers brought death on a genocidal scale to wolves across the continent. There is no doubt that the elimination of the wolf's prey—bison on the prairies, deer in eastern Canada—contributed to the wolf's demise. And it's not as if the wolf was the only predator singled out for slaughter. In what naturalist Barry Lopez calls an ''American pogrom,'' millions of predatory creatures, from the black-footed ferret to the bald eagle, were exterminated.

Where localized hunting didn't remove the wolf, governments established bounty systems to encourage the killing. In 1909 in British Columbia, trappers were paid $2.50 for each wolf killed. By 1949, the price for a wolf had risen to $40. Similar rates existed elsewhere. During its peak period in the late 1940s, 10 000 wolves per year were being killed in Canada for bounties. The bounty system was supplemented in many places with mass poisonings of wolves. Ranchers in Texas would lace pieces of meat with cyanide or strychnine and trappers in the Yukon would set out poisoned bait.

These methods of eliminating the North American wolf population ceased around 1960. But by that time, the wolf had become virtually extinct in nearly half its former territory. Except for the tiny enclaves of wolves in the American south and Mexico and the 1200 or so timber wolves that survived in northern Minnesota, the contiguous 48 states are practically free of wolves even today. Fewer than 100 wolves live in the northern-tier states along

LEFT: *Alaskan wolf biologist Gordon Haber likens the killing of a dominant adult wolf to the killing of a respected elder in a human clan. Removing the depository of the group's knowledge—for wolves the den-sites, trails, hunting strategies, and interpack behavior—incapacitates the survivors.*

Chetco Community Public Library

the Canadian border. A rough line, drawn east to west through Canada 50 to 100 kilometres (30 to 60 miles) north of the U.S. border, marks the southern border of the remaining territory of large numbers of wolves in North America. It is estimated that 60 000 wolves still live in Canada, the largest surviving group in the world. Another 6000 wolves live in Alaska.

In the last few decades, public attitudes toward the wolf—and the steady decline in the wolf population—have, in most places, been reversed. Part of this is due to the belated realization that in the U.S. the wolf was headed toward extinction. Better management of the wolf's prey population and the end of bounties and poisonings have allowed *Canis lupus* to re-establish itself in some regions where it had disappeared. With the exception of the Mexican wolf, all remaining subspecies of North American wolf are now increasing in number.

But more than the changes in game management and legislation, the public itself has found in the wolf a modern-day metaphor for nature untrammeled by human predation. People who know the wolf best—backcountry hikers, outfitters, natives, naturalists—return from the continent's fast-disappearing wilderness bearing a message about the wolf quite different than the one borne by frontiersmen and farmers of generations past. Those who know the wolf most intimately speak in awe of the wolf's parental skills: feeding, playing, instructing, and disciplining the pups in a communal family of parents and older siblings. The human visitors among the wolf have come to admire the sophistication and tenacity the pack employs, working as a team to track and subdue its prey. Despite centuries of persecution for their predations of livestock, modern research has shown this occurs, in fact, infrequently. In a 1981

PREVIOUS PAGE: *The wolf's world is bridged by the tactile vocabulary of nuzzles, sniffs, pawing, and rubbing. Every pack is a well-established hierarchy. The lower-ranking wolves—like courtiers in a medieval court—perform ritual displays of subservience, literally bowing before and licking the dominant wolves.*

RIGHT: *Among wolves, as in human society, certain creatures do not easily fit in. Sometimes the weakest animal in a pack, sometimes the loser of a fight, sometimes a young, aggressive male is ostracized and driven away. As among* Homo sapiens, *this wolf heads into unknown territory—often covering vast distances—until it finds a new place to call home.*

Minnesota study, it was calculated that wolves killed 110 sheep and 30 cattle that year out of a state-wide population of livestock numbering 300 000.

Those who have lived among wolves are inevitably impressed by the sociability among pack members: the nuzzling, sniffing, rubbing, wrestling, the helping of injured members, the protectiveness toward the babies. They are, as well, inevitably struck by the wolf's amazing skills in navigation, marking trails, defending its territory's perimeter, wandering long distances daily before returning home to the den. Outdoors, at night, wherever the wolf still survives, the eerie yowling—first one voice, then two, then a chorus of undulating, lugubrious howls—reminds those who have heard the sound that the darkness is still alive with possibilities. The wolf's forlorn cries alert humankind to the precariousness of nature's creatures and the mystical quality of wilderness.

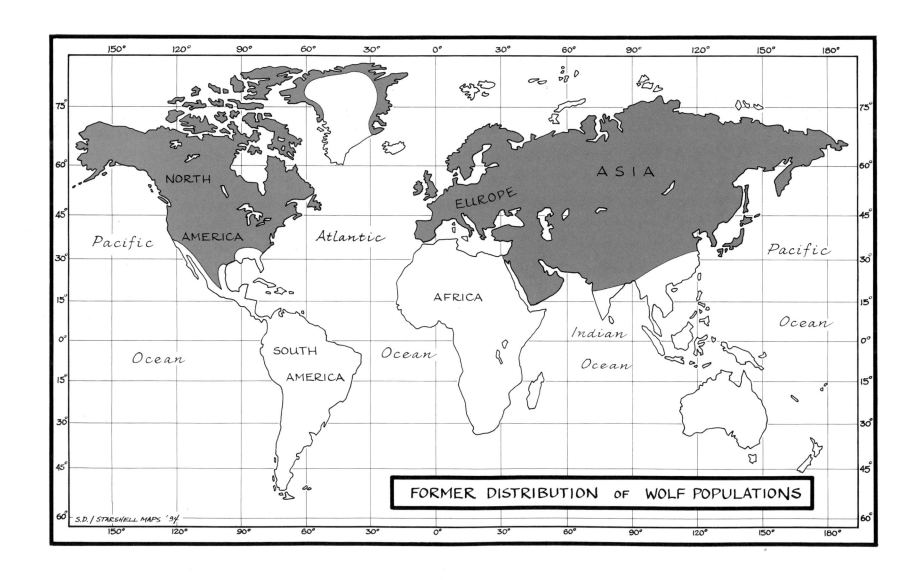

FORMER DISTRIBUTION OF WOLF POPULATIONS

S.D. / STARSHELL MAPS '94

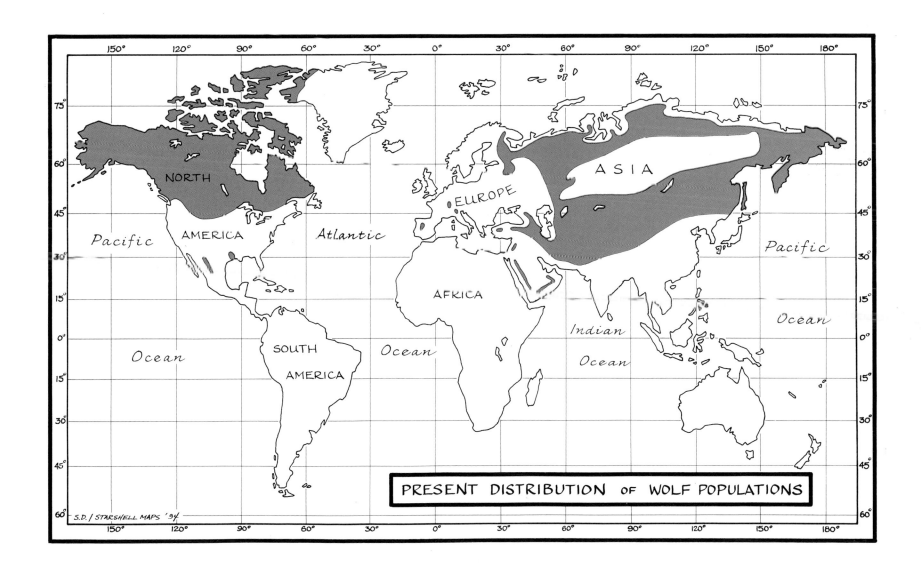

PRESENT DISTRIBUTION OF WOLF POPULATIONS

S.D./STARSHELL MAPS '94

LEFT: *As the snowline descends toward the gravelly, willow-lined stream beds of the arctic each autumn, the wolf may pursue its favored northern prey, the caribou, over vast distances. These caribou-hunting wolves are the only ones not to have an established territory, migrating instead along with the migrating herds.*

RIGHT: *Among groups of wolves in North America, physical size, diet, number of animals in the pack, and coloration vary considerably. The arctic wolf is often whitish-gray. The timber wolf in most of Canada and northern Minnesota ranges from jet black through gray to tawny. The red wolf and Mexican wolf have, especially on the ears and haunches, an auburn color.*

ABOVE: *From the earliest arrival of the colonial settlers in North America, the wolf has been demonized and persecuted. By 1850 it had been eradicated from most of the northeast. By 1900 it had—with the exception of northern Minnesota—disappeared from the American midwest. By 1950 it had become virtually extinct throughout the western United States.*

ABOVE: *A gray wolf, its ears alert, stalks its prey at the edge of a forest-enclosed meadow. When not sleeping or socializing, the wolf roams relentlessly, often covering up to 25 kilometres (15 miles) a day in pursuit of food.*

RIGHT: *The boreal forests of Canada are home to a high percentage of the world's remaining wolves. Rich in deer, elk, moose, and numerous smaller creatures such as beavers and geese, the vast forests provide the wolf with sufficient nourishment and isolation from human predators that—unlike almost everywhere else—the wolf population of Canada has never faced extirpation.*

LEFT: *As the sedges of the arctic tundra turn honey-colored and the fireweed withers each September, the gray wolf faces the annual prospect of diminished prey. The onset of winter, for the wolf and for most of North America's wild animals, is the time the weak and young are most likely to die.*

ABOVE: *The wolf is a skilled hunter, depending on its nose and speed to detect and subdue its prey. It can trot for half a day at eight kilometres per hour (five miles per hour) and in short, five- to ten-minute bursts achieve a speed of 65 kilometres per hour (40 miles per hour). It will often run ungulates, such as deer and elk, to exhaustion before moving in for the kill.*

LEFT: *This wolf's muzzle attracts a fly to the lingering bloodstain from a recent kill. Like its relative the dog, wolves are fond of rolling in anything smelly, apparently happy to acquire the wild perfume of old blood, excrement, or decay.*

LEFT: *As winter approaches in the Rocky Mountains, the wolf here—as elsewhere in North America—faces a time of deprivation and possible death. The amount of available food decreases. The cold increases the chance of death among the young and weak. Some native Americans say the cries of a solitary wolf are from the lost souls of the human dead trying to return to earth.*

ABOVE: *The ritual marking of territorial boundaries and trails is part of the wolf's daily life. The pack's exclusive control of its domain remains stable, often through generations. It is defended against interlopers first by scent-marking trees, rocks, bushes, and stumps and, if necessary, by attacking—or killing— intruders. The wolf here rubs its lips and cheek on a tree to caution outsiders they have entered ''foreign'' territory.*

RIGHT: *With the first frosts of late August, the arctic tundra undergoes a metamorphosis. The shrubs and trees are suddenly lit by an inner fire as the greens transform to magenta, jasmine, mauve, copper, and henna. This wolf sits on its haunches, hoping to detect the movement of some small animal amid the carpet of colors.*

ABOVE: *In the glaciated wasteland of Canada's Ellesmere Island, fewer than 1000 kilometres (600 miles) from the North Pole, this pack of white arctic wolves searches for prey by the light of an endless summer day. If they are very fortunate, they'll locate a herd of musk ox. If less fortunate, a rabbit. But research has shown that wolves can, if circumstances require it, go days or weeks—even a month —without eating a thing.*

LEFT: *On occasion, wolves kill their own kind. Sometimes a fight within a pack will result in fatal injuries. More often, as here, a lone female timber wolf was killed by a pack protecting its territory against the intruder.*

LEFT: *As Canadian wolf expert John Theberge wrote, "Wolves fear humans for good reason. Humans fear wolves out of misunderstanding." Only in the past 35 years has the gray wolf population stabilized in North America, recently showing signs of increase in areas of the northern United States.*

ABOVE: *The wolf's vocabulary includes yips, squeaks, whimpers, barks, growls, snarls, and, of course, howls. Most howling occurs as part of pack behavior, the wolves chorusing together, ranging through notes and octaves for several minutes. Naturalists have reported hearing a solitary wolf howl in apparent grief after the death of its mate. Despite a widespread belief to the contrary, wolves do not howl at the moon.*

SOCIAL BEHAVIOR

DANCING WITH WOLVES: A YEAR IN THE LIFE OF A PACK

In the lowland forests of south Texas, where sweet gum grows along the creeks feeding the Sabine River, there are—it seems—no wolves. In the mosquito-filled second-growth forest of Isle Royale, set like an eye in wolfhead-shaped Lake Superior, there are plenty of deer in the jack pine along the ridges and the quaking aspen along the stream beds. But again: no wolves to be seen. In the Yukon, where the willows turn jasmine on the flanks of the Ogilvie Mountains with the first September frost: no apparent wolves.

There *are* wolves: a few hundred in Texas, a few dozen on Isle Royale, a few thousand in the Yukon. But the society of wolves prefers wilderness, vast territories far from the dangers posed by the society of man. The wolf is one of the shyest of large North American animals. It is seldom seen. It usually prefers to hunt in the twilight of early morning and dusk and to sleep during the midday hours. A decade ago, for example, among 15 000 visitors to Isle

PREVIOUS PAGE, LEFT: *This gray wolf pup still shows its youth in its oversized paws and downy fur.*

PREVIOUS PAGE, RIGHT: *About three weeks before the pregnant wolf will give birth, she digs a den, often in a high site offering both a good vantage point and secure surroundings. Rocky crevices, tree stumps, sandy ridges, or rock piles are preferred. The den's 60-centimetre-wide (two-foot) tunnel opens under-ground into a larger chamber. Sixty-three days after conception, the mother wolf gives birth, typically to 6 to 11 pups. Some dens have shown more or less continuous occupation for 100 years.*

Royale National Park in one year, there were just a dozen reported sightings of a wolf.

For most people who venture into the remote places where the wolf still survives, their only contact with this mythic creature may be the sound of distant, eerie yowling. The wolf does not howl at the moon. But it may be drawn into howling by the sound of a passing train's whistle, a loon's call, or the faraway buzz of a chainsaw. Mostly, though, a wolf pack howls in happiness or apprehension, joining in as one member celebrates a fresh kill or a lost member cries out for directions or a second pack howls threateningly nearby. Each pack has its own distinctive chorus, the individual wolves harmonizing like members of a melancholic barbershop quartet. This strange "yow-ooh-yowing" lasts typically from one to

LEFT: *Young wolves soon learn the intricacies of pack behavior. Inevitably low in the hierarchy, the young acquire submissive traits and expressions. They keep their fangs sheathed and their posture low, legs slightly bent, tail curled under their rump, almost cringing. They keep their eyes narrowed and averted from dominant adults, their ears flattened and their hackles smooth. They learn to lick and nuzzle obsequiously the higher-ranking wolves.*

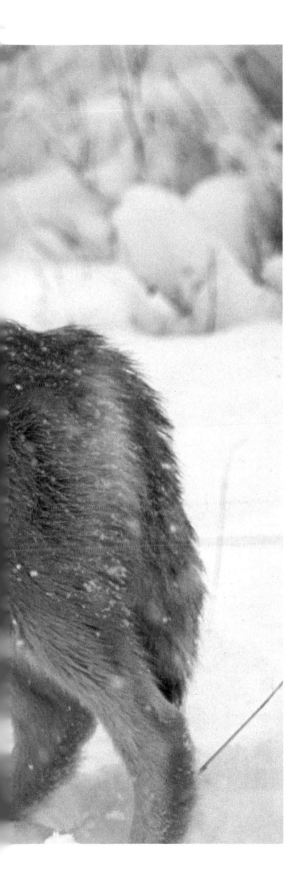

five minutes and on a still night in the treeless arctic tundra can be heard over an area of 250 square kilometres (100 square miles).

This howling, though the best known, is probably the least important of the wolf's methods of communication. Like most predators, the wolf lives in a world populated by *smells*. Its compulsive scent-marking—urinating on stumps, rocks, kill-sites, and intersections of woodland trails; rubbing its body scent on trees, its dead prey, and each other—link members of a pack together through their noses. These same odors, when encountered by an intruder, usually cause the stranger to retreat hastily.

The hierarchy within the pack is communicated not only by these olfactory clues, but also by body postures and facial expressions. From its earliest age, a wolf pup learns that submission is conveyed by a skulking posture, head lowered, eyes averted, ears flattened, mouth closed. Conversely, the baring of fangs, a fixed stare, and the raising of ears and hackles means trouble—and a possible fight. In the society of wolves, these expressions, motions, and scent-markings are ritualized, understood by all, and help reinforce pack cohesion.

This cohesion gets tested in the late winter each year as the annual breeding season approaches. When the pack's dominant female—known in scientific jargon as the alpha female—reaches estrus, fighting is common. The males, especially the dominant alpha male, sniff, pursue, and harass the breeding female, hoping she'll yield. The alpha female, meanwhile, asserts her authority in the group by fighting with the subservient females. It is a raucous time. Snarling and howling crescendo during this period. In most cases, as the viciousness

RIGHT: The nine gray wolves gather here in a winter howling session, a common feature of pack activity during the breeding season. One wolf begins yowling: "wow — oooh — wow — oooh — wow" or "yieee — eee — eee." It is then joined by others harmonizing, each wolf changing tone and tune like the members of a morose glee club. In most cases, despite the traditional imagery, wolves don't sit when they howl. They stand.

PREVIOUS PAGE: While the idea that wolves mate for life holds a strong appeal among human observers, it's not necessarily so. The death of a dominant wolf requires a new coupling. Fights and injuries may produce a new hierarchy, too, as dominance shifts to a younger animal. There is usually a strong bond between dominant pairs, but it's not always monogamous.

reaches its peak, the dominant pair decide to retain their long partnership and mate. Despite a widespread belief otherwise, paired wolves aren't necessarily monogamous. Changes in partners do occur, but infrequently. In most packs—the exception is very large groups of 15 or 20—none of the other adults will mate and produce a litter.

Sixty-three days after conception (the same gestation period as dogs), the pups are born underground—in February or March in Texas and as late as June on the arctic tundra. For the first two weeks, the pups are blind, living in darkness, suckling and sleeping. After about three weeks, the pups are carried out the den's tunnel in their mother's mouth to learn about the world. Solid food, in the form of regurgitated chunks of half-digested meat, is part of the pups' initiation into life above ground. Older siblings help the parents, baby-sitting, bringing food, serving as convenient jungle-gyms for the pack's only set of children.

Naturalists report that this is invariably a joyful time for the pack. The wolf pups—like all puppies—frolic endlessly, fuzzy balls of energy constantly testing the adults' patience. The babies sniff, they nuzzle, they lick, they wag, they nip at their litter-mates, wrestling and yipping in their undeveloped squeaky voices. They harass their ever-tolerant uncles and aunts and parents. They fight over the chunks of prechewed meat brought to them, imitating the snarling and quarreling that accompanies some adult meals.

As the pups mature, they are taken farther afield and introduced to the trails, scents, potential prey, and strategies of pack-hunting. The pups quickly learn to identify the adults' cautionary growls and snarls. Naturalists have watched adults begin a hunt, then abruptly

relinquish the chase to the youngsters, observing how well they've mastered the craft of appraising the prey's vulnerability and how well they close for the kill.

By October, the pups are almost fully grown and participating completely in pack life. Some remain with the pack until death, typically at about nine years of age. Some depart after a year or two and become "lone wolves," often traveling vast distances in search of a mate. This is a treacherous time, since established wolf packs may injure or kill intruders.

But if one lone wolf is fortunate, there's a second skulking around, trying to avoid attack and find a partner. With the cessation of bounties and poisoning of wolves and the ban on hunting in many areas, the wolf's range is gradually spreading outward as new packs are formed by these wanderers. As well, the governments of some states and provinces are starting to resettle packs in established wilderness areas currently devoid of wolves. There may come a time early in the 21st century when the wolf pack's mournful call of the wild will reverberate again across the dark hills and rolling plains of North America, in places that have been silent now for centuries.

LEFT: *This dominant alpha male holds the muzzle of a subservient wolf in its jaws. Such actions assert the high-ranking male's authority and so prevent fights. Cautionary behavior peaks each winter as pack males vie for the attention of the alpha female. The rivalry occurs in December among the most southerly wolves and in April on the islands of the high arctic.*

ABOVE: *As autumn turns to winter and the breeding season approaches, wolf packs turn snarly. Fights are common. The most vicious fighter is usually the dominant alpha female, whose attacks on low-ranking pack members may cause injuries. Here the dominant female (on the left) shows evidence she's in estrus—blood near the base of her tail. In most packs, only the dominant female will produce a litter.*

LEFT: *This white alpha male mounts his gray partner while a black-furred, third member of the pack stands nearby. These coloration differences— even within a small pack—are not uncommon.*

RIGHT: *After all the sexually inspired hullabaloo, the established pair-bonds are usually maintained. Here the alpha male tries to coax a reluctant alpha female with his foot. At other times, the dominant female may be the aggressive one, urinating near the dominant male to encourage him to mate.*

LEFT: *These three arctic wolf pups are interested in what their mother is carrying inside her. With a lot of shoving and nuzzling, the young are rewarded with a bit of recently devoured meat, regurgitated from their mother's stomach.*

ABOVE: *Part of the social order depends on ritual baring of teeth. This alpha female asserts her authority over an intimidated, younger female. Sometimes these altercations turn violent. On occasion, the dominant female may be deposed. She may then be ostracized by the pack and forced to flee, becoming a renegade lone wolf.*

ABOVE: *These week-old timber wolves show all the vulnerability of most other young mammals. They are fuzzy, rotund, helpless, and blind. For two weeks, they can't see. Until they begin to be weaned toward the end of their first month, they will live entirely underground, sleeping and suckling.*

RIGHT: *By the end of their first year, the young wolves are participating in all the pack's activities, including such proper social etiquette as fawning over higher-ranking wolves. Here a pair of year-old wolves demonstrates appropriate subservient nuzzling behavior toward an adult. As the young grow, they also join the rest of the pack on hunting expeditions, abandoning the ''rendezvous site'' for lengthy trips.*

ABOVE: *Gradually the mother introduces the pups to solid food: pieces of meat regurgitated in a bird-like manner for the babies to consume. The father, too, helps out in parenting, tending and feeding the pups. It doesn't take long for the babies to develop more wolf-like features: rounded ears become more pointed; noses elongate; legs lengthen.*

LEFT: *As the pups mature, they're gradually weaned. Here a three-week-old timber wolf pup gets a little mid-air refuelling before returning to play. Wolf pups amuse themselves in frantic half-hour bursts of running, tumbling, yipping, tail-wagging, wrestling, and nuzzling followed by equally intense periods of sleeping.*

RIGHT: *As some lupine blooms beside the mouth of a den, a trio of pups has emerged into the daylight world. Here the young are initiated into pack behavior. They learn to respond to their parent's cautionary growls and nips. They develop a taste for meat, gnawing on bones brought them by adults. They learn the parameters of their terrestrial "rendezvous site," an area of about 1000 square metres (1200 square yards) that serves as their above-ground home until they're old enough to go out on hunts.*

LEFT: *A young gray wolf sits near its summer den on a rocky bluff practicing its howl. As the wolf matures, its voice deepens from barking ''yip-yips'' to more throaty ''yow — ooohs.''*

FAR LEFT: *Wolf pups are usually treated with forbearance and affection by all members of the pack. Since only one pair of adult wolves in each pack typically breeds, the puppies are viewed as communal babies.*

LEFT: *The wolf is among the most sociable mammals on earth. For members of the pack, contact takes the form of sniffing, nuzzling, play-fighting, tail-wagging, nipping, and napping together. Each animal knows the smell and hierarchical position of the other and pays constant attention to the little actions that unite the group.*

ABOVE: *Feeding a growing family of wolf pups is a big job. Often the entire pack helps since there is usually only one litter per pack. Returning adults are inevitably greeted by the pups with an over-zealous show of affection, each one tumbling and climbing over the others in a scramble to get first dibs at—as here— a freshly delivered deer leg. A sure sign of a wolf's den-site is a sprinkling of gnawed bones on the ground.*

RIGHT: *As the pups mature, they explore the surrounding forest and tundra in ever-widening circuits. Here a young wolf crosses a river. Nearly half of all young wolves die in their first year: the result of fights, disease, inexperience, hunting accidents, and the occasional attacks of other predators, such as grizzlies and polar bears.*

ABOVE: *The wolf incessantly marks its territory, rubbing and urinating on objects along its perimeter. These boundaries are usually strictly observed by members of other packs. Some naturalists have observed a pack of wolves chasing a deer until it crossed into a second pack's domain. Suddenly, the chase ceased. The pursuing pack preferred to abandon their prey rather than confront the other pack.*

RIGHT: *An alpha female scent-marks using the raised-leg urination position while four subservient males watch. Regardless of sex, dominant wolves urinate using the raised-leg position; low-ranking wolves of either sex use the squatting urination position. Lone wolves and those trying to minimize any appearance of aggressiveness employ the squatting position since it limits the range their scent is likely to travel.*

RIGHT: *This year-old timber wolf adds a few more gnaw-marks to the whitening antlers of an elk. The wolf is now fully grown and may stay with its birth pack or strike out as a lone wolf, attempting to establish its own pack.*

ABOVE: *On a barren, windswept ridge on Ellesmere Island in Canada's high arctic, a pack of white wolves considers attacking a herd of musk ox. A young wolf, inexperienced in confrontations with dangerous prey like moose or musk ox, is sometimes overzealous in its approach. A lunge from the horns or a kick from the hooves of one of these musk ox can be fatal.*

HUNTING IN THE WILDERNESS

THE WOLF'S TOOTH:
THE KILLER SHAPES THE PREY

The wolf hunts first with its nose, then with its feet, and last with its four-centimetre (1.5-inch) fangs. Armed with an extraordinary sense of smell, equal to or better than any dog's, it can detect the faintest whiff of a deer or seal or caribou 2.5 kilometres (1.5 miles) distant. Once alerted to the possibility of prey, members of the pack gather to sniff the air, their ears upright, their tails wagging in anticipation, waiting for a signal that a hunt is about to begin. Led usually by the dominant alpha male, the pack forms a sort of furred posse, following their leader single-file along well-established trails in pursuit of the scent.

Despite its reputation as a team of lethal predators, in 90 percent of these forays the wolf pack does not catch its intended victim. Deer invariably scatter. A moose may run or it may stand and fight, occasionally inflicting fatal wounds on its attackers. Musk ox form a circular wall of lowered horns and sharp hooves, their young protected within. Facing such situa-

PREVIOUS PAGE, LEFT: *These two arctic wolves follow a trail across a frozen Alaskan lake. All wolves' territories are criss-crossed by such well-trodden trails: the snow compacted, the intersections regularly scent-marked with urine, the routes often leading toward regular kill-sites.*

PREVIOUS PAGE, RIGHT: *Once an animal is killed, the pack often fights over the spoils, threatening to inflict injury on each other with their fangs. This expression—black lips pulled back revealing danger-ous canine teeth, the hair on the forehead and hackles up-right—cautions the wolf's opponents around the fallen prey that it is about to bite.*

tions, the pack often taunts and tests the prey, feinting and then retreating to study the animals' reactions. If the herd or an individual flees, the pack tags along, assessing its chances of success. An injured elk, a musk ox calf, an old, disease-weakened moose present the least risk of injury to the wolves and the most chance of a kill. A wolf pack may trail the animal for hours, days even, sometimes over long distances, waiting for the right moment, the right terrain. In this way, the wolf culls the prey and, in Darwinian terms, assures that the fastest and strongest survive to reproduce. This is what American poet Robinson Jeffers meant when he wrote: *What but the wolf's tooth whittled so fine/ The fleet limbs of the antelope.*

Depending on the type of animal and the terrain, the pack employs a variety of tactics. Sometimes decoys are deployed upwind, provoking the prey to flee directly into an ambush. Sometimes the prey is run to exhaustion. Sometimes the pack surrounds its prey, driving a herd into the open where the most vulnerable individual can then be picked off.

The first bite is often to the prey's head, ear, or nose. Other members of the pack lunge at its legs, flanks, and hamstrings, trying to cripple the animal. The intended victim may elude

LEFT: *This white wolf has caught an arctic hare. The islands of Canada's high north are bleak, almost desert-like, and—for much of the year— unimaginably cold. The wolf's prey is limited by the climate. Ptarmigan, voles, Old Squaw ducks, lemmings, and rabbits provide sustenance when musk ox and caribou can't be found.*

the whittling of the wolf's tooth for a while, leaving a trail of blood which the pack follows. The end usually comes quickly—within minutes of the first bite. The weakened prey relinquishes the fight, collapses, and is set upon in a bloody frenzy of canine teeth.

The reality of the wolf's existence is that it's often hungry. It is not uncommon for a pack to go days without a kill. When the pack does manage to catch its prey, the victim is quickly eviscerated and eaten with an enthusiasm that has little to do with decorum. The wolves snarl and fight viciously among themselves: black lips baring white fangs; muzzles stained red with blood; mouths gulping down 10 kilograms (22 pounds) of meat in a single orgy of eating. What doesn't get consumed at the kill-site will be, in time, lugged piecemeal back to the denning area where it's either distributed to the pups or buried for future feasts.

These major kills are frequently supplemented with a diet of fortuitously found appetizers: a ptarmigan, a vole, a snake, even grubs, berries, and road-kills. No one has ever accused the wolf of being a fussy eater. There have been, as well, documented cases of wolves killing for fun. Occasionally among domestic livestock or in situations of abundance, naturalists report the instinctive hunting ability of the pack, something seen also among foxes, hyenas, and sea gulls, is aroused to indiscriminate attack. It's as if the excitement of pursuit and capture, a trait the human species has raised to a tragic art, runs in the veins of some predators and finds release in momentary bloodthirstiness. Mostly, though, the wolf lives precariously, an elusive and shadowy reminder that every predator dances with violence and that the canine tooth is—by design—meant to bite.

RIGHT: *In a study of wolf predation on Isle Royale in Lake Superior, a wolf pack discerned—by smell or sight— over 100 moose. Most out- fought or outran the pack, but seven were caught. Six moose died; one escaped with in- juries. The wolves' success rate in this study was less than 6 percent.*

PREVIOUS PAGE: *Despite centu- ries of persecution for their occasional killing of domestic animals, wolves seldom attack cattle and sheep, preferring instead wild game. In a three-year study in British Columbia, wolves killed on average 200 domestic animals annually, two-thirds of these calves and lambs. The average financial loss to all B.C. farmers and ranchers from wolf attacks was $22 000 a year. Here a pack of B.C. wolves rips into the intes- tines of its favored prey—a mule deer.*

ABOVE: *Throughout their North American territory, ravens often accompany wolves, hoping to garner leftovers. In fact, flocks of ravens have been observed teasing wolves. Some of the flock position themselves just beyond the wolves' jaws, taunting the wolves to abandon the kill temporarily so that other ravens can quickly descend and sneak a furtive morsel.*

LEFT: *The 300-kilogram (650-pound) musk ox of Canada's high arctic are formidable foes for wolves. When threatened, the herd forms a defensive circle, offering horns and powerful hooved kicks to their attackers. Usually, the wolf pack—through false charges, stare-downs and nips at an exposed flank—hopes to provoke a stampede. This may expose the youngest and weakest animal to an assault from the entire pack.*

ABOVE: *The three wolves chasing this herd of musk ox have a strategy: to drive them toward a fourth wolf. The pack has assessed the most vulnerable creature—the young musk ox at left. As the herd scatters, the wolves will lunge at the calf, sinking fangs into its head, neck, and rump. It will soon cease struggling and the wolves' muzzles and legs will be covered in blood. Within a few hours, it will be little more than a skeleton.*

RIGHT: *Here in the Rocky Mountains, as across much of Canada, deer are the wolf's main prey. On average, a wolf pack consumes the equivalent of one deer a week. In the ratio of ungulate weights, one caribou is equal to two deer and one moose is equal to six deer.*

LEFT: *Large game is usually hunted by packs. But, on occasion, especially during the summer when prey is plentiful and packs are sometimes dispersed, individual wolves do hunt deer and moose alone. Wolves often supplement their diet with small animals encountered during daily forays. Here a timber wolf scouts a springtime beaver pond.*

FAR LEFT: *These 10 timber wolves follow their leader through deep Canadian snow. In the initial stages of a hunt, this military style approach is often employed—with one wolf breaking trail while the rest trot dutifully behind. As the pack nears its prey, the tempo increases. The wolves will then frequently spread out, forming a moving phalanx of fangs.*

LEFT: *Seven gray wolves gorge themselves on a white-tailed deer. Wolves often wear on their muzzles the bloody red badge of conquest as they eviscerate their victim. It's not uncommon for each wolf to devour almost a dozen kilograms (25 pounds) of meat— sometimes a third of their body weight—in one frenzy of eating. In Minnesota, one small pack of wolves ate an entire 400-kilogram (900-pound) moose in one week.*

ABOVE: *In a fjord on the coast of Ellesmere Island, located west of Greenland, an arctic wolf pauses on the floating remnant of an iceberg, studying the water for the movement of a seal or fish.*

RIGHT: *A post-dinner drink follows the wolf's meal. The blood is washed away. The stomach feels full. There's no immediate need to hunt.*

LEFT: *In most regions it inhabits, the wolf lives at the top of the food chain: the hunter, not the hunted. Its only serious danger—now, as in the past—is from humans, who trap and hunt for furs or cull for game management purposes. Since the wolf detects its animal prey primarily with its nose, its victims may not notice the silent approach of a pair of predatory yellow eyes.*

ABOVE: *Little is left of this musk ox kill except for its ribs and horns. These two wolves will clean the bones on this Ellesmere Island ridge until not a scrap of meat is left.*

LEFT: *Despite a reputation for voraciousness, the wolf is hungry most of the time. In fact, only 10 percent of its attempts to kill prey are successful. This situation forces the wolf to roam almost continuously, hoping to arrive downwind from an unsuspecting deer or rabbit. Using a radio collar, naturalists tracked one wolf for a year and found it ranged over an area of 5000 square kilometres (2000 square miles).*

LEFT: *The wolf is capable of running in bursts of incredible speed as it closes on its prey. The chase is usually brief—a few minutes. Many animals elude their attackers, but the wolf has enormous patience and stamina. The members of a pack may take turns chasing the prey, until it collapses in exhaustion.*

ABOVE: *This ten-month-old wolf has joined the pack in the kill of a white-tailed deer. Once every member of the pack has eaten—and the most subservient frequently eat last—the pack's members often take a snooze to recover from the combined effects of the chase and the feast.*

EPILOGUE

THE WOLF RETURNS:
WILDERNESS REGAINED

One hundred years ago, the wolf was in retreat everywhere across western North America. It had already been eliminated throughout the eastern half of the continent. In 1894, nature writer Ernest Thompson Seton hunted down the "Currumpaw Wolf" of New Mexico and its mate, "Blanca." His subsequent book, *Lobo, King of the Currumpaw,* described his killing of the pair, one case among millions that illustrated the tragic slaughter of wolves in the U.S. and Canada. Three years later, wildlife artist Frederic Remington painted *Moonlight Wolf.* The painting depicted a lone Great Plains wolf, a subspecies that would—within a few years—become extinct. Across the west, bounty-hunters (called "wolfers" in the trade) shot, trapped, poisoned, and snared virtually every wolf in the western United States. Where wolves fought back, small armies of wolfers gathered. The last wolf in South Dakota, named "Three Toes" because it had barely escaped from a steel-jawed trap, was

PREVIOUS PAGE, LEFT: *Although dog owners may object, there's good evidence the wolf's intelligence is superior to its canine relatives. Over a thousand generations separate today's wolves from the early domesticated dog. The price dogs have paid for befriending humankind appears to be a decrease in their ability to navigate, work cooperatively, hunt, and survive in the wilderness by their wits alone.*

PREVIOUS PAGE, RIGHT: *This gray wolf, one of an estimated 6000 in Alaska, is hunting amid willows in Denali National Park. In the mid-1990s, scores of wolves were killed in the region just south of the park. This cull was part of a widely criticized state program aimed at helping Alaska's caribou recover from a series of severe winters. The wolf kill meant more caribou would be available to local hunters. Similar culls have recently occurred in western Canada.*

killed in 1925 after 150 men pursued it, each trying to collect as a reward a gold watch.

It wasn't until the 1960s that the tide began to turn. But by that time, some subspecies had been annihilated and others verged on extinction. Across the 48 contiguous American states, scientists searched for wolves and—with the exception of Minnesota's northern wilderness—found none. In 1962, Canadian writer Farley Mowat published his fictional account of life among the wolf, entitled *Never Cry Wolf*. It marked a watershed. The book's appearance coincided with the beginning of the environmental movement and a growing consciousness that entire species and ecosystems were threatened by human predation and pollution.

Within a few years, governments that had been paying $40 bounties on dead wolves were passing Endangered Species legislation to protect wolf habitats and wolves. By the mid-1970s, some of the few survivors of the most endangered groups of wolves—the red wolf, the

LEFT: *The only wolves to survive the 300-year-long slaughter in the lower 48 United States found sanctuary in the lake-filled wilderness of Minnesota's north. Today, the 1200 or so wolves there account for about 90 percent of the wolves south of the Canadian border. Here, as autumn approaches, a timber wolf wades into a Minnesota creek for a drink.*

Mexican wolf, the Rocky Mountain wolf—were caught in order to start captive-breeding programs. Subsequent attempts have been made, with only limited success, to re-establish these captive wolves in wilderness areas of the coastal American southeast and the forests of the Great Smoky Mountains. In the west, too, the wolf is now in ascendance, naturally repopulating parts of northern Washington, Idaho, Montana, and South Dakota.

This trend has been fostered by a growing appreciation that predators, as well as prey, are an intrinsic part of the natural environment. Scores of recent research projects, TV documentaries, and books about the wolf's natural history have given credence to a new, celebratory view of the long-maligned animal. This changed perception has also been aided by such popular works as the 1982 film version of *Never Cry Wolf,* the Academy Award-winning movie *Dances with Wolves,* and the immensely popular 1992 book *Women Who Run With the Wolves,* a study of the mythic elements of women's history. No longer inhabiting the nightmare world of ancient, irrational fears and legalized extermination, the wolf calls out today for the preservation of wilderness in North America and an appreciation for the beauty of things untamed.

LEFT: *A young timber wolf hunkers down amid a storm, its black fur frosted with snowflakes. Wolves sleep outside even during the most bitter winter cold. The underground dens are only used during the spring birthing and puppy-rearing time.*

LEFT: *The endangered red wolf of America's Deep South is smaller, lighter, and more spindly legged than the gray wolf. The red wolf prefers swampland, forests of long-leafed pine, and prairie scrubland. Recently, captive-breeding programs have been set up to save this animal from extinction and attempts have been made to re-establish it in the mountains of eastern Tennessee, the islands of South Carolina, and the lowland bayous of the Gulf states.*

ABOVE: *There's a horrifying beauty in the skull of a carnivore, in the revealed smoothness of bone and sharpness of teeth. Here, a timber wolf's skull shows some of its 42 teeth: the long canine fangs for biting and the flattened back molars for crunching bone and tearing off chunks of meat.*

ABOVE: *An arctic wolf surveys the frozen seascape and tundra from its vantage-point atop an iceberg grounded on the shore of Canada's Ellesmere Island. The wolf's exceptional eyesight and sense of smell can detect prey long before it knows it has been discovered.*

RIGHT: *The wolf seldom howls alone. Usually the pack howls together to celebrate a fresh kill, to warn wolves in an adjacent territory that they're too close, or to call when one member of the pack is lost. Individuals in a pack recognize the howling of the pack and competing packs learn to retreat if the chorus of a contending wolf pack erupts nearby.*

SUGGESTED READING

Brandenburg, Jim. 1988. *White Wolf: Living with an Arctic Legend.* Minocqua,
Wisconsin: Northword Press.

DeBlieu, Jan. 1991. *Meant to Be Wild: The Struggle to Save Endangered Species
Through Captive Breeding.* Golden, Colorado: Fulcrum.

Despain, D. et al. 1986. *Wildlife in Transition: Man and Nature on Yellowstone's
Northern Range.* Boulder: Roberts Rinehart.

Hasselstrom, Linda. 1992. *Land Circle: Writings Collected from the Land.* Golden,
Colorado: Fulcrum.

Hoagland, Edward. 1976. *Red Wolves and Black Bears.* New York: Random House.

Lawrence, R. D. 1986. *In Praise of Wolves.* New York: Henry Holt.

Lopez, Barry Holstun. 1978. *Of Wolves and Men.* New York: Scribner's.

Mech, L. David. 1988. *The Arctic Wolf: Living with the Pack.* Stillwater, Minnesota:
Voyageur Press.

Mowat, Farley. 1983. *Never Cry Wolf.* Toronto: McClelland and Stewart-Bantam.

Murray, John A. 1987. *Wildlife in Peril: The Endangered Mammals of Colorado.*
Boulder: Roberts Rinehart.

_____, ed. 1993. *Out Among the Wolves: Contemporary Writings on the Wolf.*
Vancouver: Whitecap Books Ltd.

O'Brien, Dan. 1988. *Spirit of the Hills.* New York: Crown.

Peterson, Rolf. 1977. *Wolf Ecology and Prey Relationships on Isle Royale.* National Park
Service Scientific Monograph Series 11.

Savage, Arthur and Candace Savage. 1981. *Wild Mammals of Western Canada.*
Saskatoon: Western Producer Prairie Books.

Savage, Candace. 1988. *Wolves.* Vancouver: Douglas & McIntyre.

Seton, Ernest Thompson. 1929. *Lives of Game Animals.* New York: Doubleday.

Young, S. P. 1946. *The Wolf in North American History.* Caldwell, Idaho: Caxton.

INDEX

PHOTO CREDITS

Jim Brandenburg/Minden Pictures 10–11, 34, 69, 72–73, 79, 86, 89, 96-97, 102

Tim Christie 1, 4–5, 24, 26–27, 28, 36, 55, 68, 95

Daniel Cox 20–21, 32–33, 42–43, 46–47, 49, 50–51, 56, 58–59, 61, 64–65, 71, 74–75, 80–81, 90–91

Dawn Goss/First Light 39

Stephen Homer/First Light 29

Thomas Kitchin/First Light 6, 12, 17, 23, 31, 62, 83, 84–85, 87, 94, 101

Aubrey Lang 38

Scott Leslie/First Light 14–15

Peter McLeod/First Light x, 8–9, 35, 45, 48, 53, 54, 57, 60, 63, 67, 77, 93, 103

L. David Mech 52, 78

Rolf Peterson 82

Lynn M. Stone vi–vii, 2–3, 22, 25, 30, 37, 40–41, 66, 70, 76, 88, 92, 98–99, 100

WITHDRAWN

Chetco Community Public Library
405 Alder Street
Brookings, OR 97415